Two Awesome Gifts For You

I want to say thanks for buying my book so I've put together two awesome free gifts for you.

The Essential Kitchen Series Cooking Hacks & Tips Book

&

100 Delicious New Recipes

These gifts are the perfect add-on to this book and I know you'll love them.

So visit the link below to grab them now!

www.GoodLivingPublishing.com/essential-kitchen

Table of Contents

Two Awesome Free Gifts For You 1
Introduction 3
Spiced Roasted Leg of Lamb 4
Roasted Leg of Lamb with Potatoes 6
Roasted Lamb Shoulder Chops 8
Roasted Rack of Lamb 10
Roasted Lamb Shank with Mashed Potatoes 11
Grilled Spicy Lamb Chops 13
Grilled Chops with Cherry Tomatoes & Asparagus 14
Grilled Leg of Lamb 16
Lamb & Carrot Soup 17
Lamb & Beans Soup 18
Lamb & Beans Soup 19
Spicy Minced Lamb with Peas 20
Baked Spicy Meatballs with Yogurt Dip 22
Meatballs in Spicy Tomato Gravy 24
Cheesy Lamb Burgers with Mayo Dip 26
Two Awesome Free Gifts For You 28

Introduction
Lamb Recipes
The Essential Kitchen Series, Book 89

Irresistible Lamb Recipes to Create Mouthwatering Meals Anyone Can Prepare at Home

Get ready to prepare a wild assortment of delicious lamb-based recipes for any meal of the day. Yes, that's right. The Essential Kitchen Series delivers an incredible assortment of lamb recipes in one quick purchase. You'll get an assortment of Lamb Recipes, which will inspire and lift any meal. They're all herein one fantastic bundle. Enjoy a host of recipes that will simplify your day, save you time, and help you enjoy something new and delicious.

This cookbook is packed with so much fun and flavor that you'll be amazed at what you can create. Just take a look at some of the unique recipes we've included:

- Roasted Lamb Shoulder Chops
- Roasted Rack of Lamb
- Roasted Lamb Shank with Mashed Potatoes

There is literally no way to go wrong with these wonderful recipes, and no better way to prepare a nutritious meal than as described in the pages of this masterful recipe collection. Inside these unusually simple guides, you'll learn how to make the most of your time, utilizing fresh ingredients and prime cuts of meat.

If you've ever wanted to step outside the norm and try something different, this is the cookbook intended for you. Where else will you learn to prepare delicious lamb chops and shanks in a single download? Bring a new blend of unique flavors into your kitchen and prepare one of these recipes today!

Spiced Roasted Leg of Lamb

Makes: 4-6 servings

Ingredients:

For Marinade:
- 2/3 cup plain Greek yogurt
- 1 tablespoon tomato puree
- 1 tablespoon fresh lemon juice
- 3-4 finely minced large garlic cloves
- 1 teaspoon finely minced fresh ginger
- 2 tablespoons chopped fresh rosemary
- 2 teaspoons ground coriander
- 1 teaspoon ground cumin
- 1 teaspoon ground cinnamon
- 1 teaspoon crushed red pepper flakes
- ¼ teaspoon sweet paprika
- ½ teaspoon ground turmeric
- Salt and freshly ground black pepper, as required
- 1 (4½-pound) bone-in leg of lamb

Procedure:

In a large bowl, add yogurt, tomato puree, lemon juice, garlic cloves, ginger, rosemary, coriander, cumin, cinnamon, red pepper flakes, paprika, turmeric, salt and black pepper and mix till well combined. Add leg of lamb and coat with marinade generously.

Cover and refrigerate to marinate for 8 to 10 hours, flipping occasionally. Remove the marinated leg of lamb from refrigerator and keep at room temperature before roasting.

Preheat the oven to 425 degree F. Line a large roasting pan with greased foil paper. Arrange the leg of lamb into prepared roasting pan. Roast for 20 minutes.

Remove the roasting pan from oven and change the side of leg of lamb. Now, reduce the temperature of oven to 325 degree F. Roast for 40 minutes. Now loosely cover the roasting pan with a large foil paper. Roast for 40 minutes more.

Roasted Leg of Lamb with Potatoes

Makes: 8 servings

Ingredients:

For Marinade:
- 1 cup red wine
- ¼ cup olive oil
- 8 finely chopped garlic cloves
- 2 teaspoons finely grated lime zest
- 1 tablespoon crushed dried rosemary
- 1 tablespoon crushed dried oregano
- Salt and freshly ground black pepper, as needed
- 1 (6-pound) bone-in leg of lamb

For Rub Mixture:
- 6 crushed garlic cloves
- 1 tablespoon crushed dried rosemary
- 1 tablespoon crushed dried oregano
- 1 tablespoon Dijon mustard
- Salt and freshly ground black pepper, as needed
- 2 tablespoons olive oil

For Potatoes:
- 20-24 small potatoes, scrubbed
- 2 tablespoons olive oil

Procedure:

For marinade in a large bowl, add red wine, olive oil, garlic cloves, lime zest, rosemary, oregano, salt and black pepper and mix till well combined.

Add leg of lamb and coat with marinade generously. Cover and refrigerate to marinate for 8 to 10 hours, flipping occasionally. Preheat the oven to 375 degrees F. Remove the marinated leg of lamb from refrigerator. For rub mixture in another large bowl, add crushed garlic, , rosemary, oregano, Dijon mustard, salt and black peppers and mix till well combined.

Remove the marinated leg of lamb from refrigerator. Remove leg of lamb from marinade. Safe the remaining marinade. With the tip of a sharp knife, make cuts in several places. Rub the mixture over lamb generously, pressing into cuts. Drizzle with oil.

Place leg of limb on a rack in a large shallow roasting pan. Add potatoes in the bowl of reserved marinade. Add oil and toss to coat well. Arrange potatoes and marinade around the leg of lamb. Roast for about 1½ hours. Flip the side of lamb and stir the potatoes. Roast for 45 minutes more.

Roasted Lamb Shoulder Chops

Makes: 4 servings

Ingredients:

- 1 tablespoon canola oil
- 4 (8-10-ounce) lamb shoulder blade chops
- Salt and freshly ground black pepper, as required
- 4 large sprigs fresh rosemary
- 2 cups plusred wine
- 3-ounce finely chopped dried apricots
- 3-ounce finely chopped dried plums
- 2 tablespoons cubed, chilled unsalted butter
- 1 tablespoon minced fresh rosemary

Procedure:

In a large skillet, heat oil on medium heat. Add lamb chops. Sprinkle with a little salt and black pepper. Sear the lamb chops for 1 minute per side.

Transfer the chops into a large plate. Keep aside for about 5 minutes to cool. In a large sealable bag, add lamb chops rosemary sprigs and wine. Arrange the bag in a large container and refrigerate to marinate for at least 3 to 4 hours.

Preheat the oven to 250 degrees F. Remove the container from refrigerator. Transfer the chops with marinade in a 10-inch oven proof pan. Cover the pan and place on the middle rack of the oven. Roast for about 3½ hours. Transfer the chops into a plate, cover with a foil paper to keep them warm.

Discard the rosemary sprigs from gravy. Through a strainer, strain 2 cups of the liquid into a pan. Place the pan on medium-low heat. Stir in apricots and plums. Cook, beating occasionally for about 8 to 10 minutes or till sauce thickened.

Gradually, add butter cubes, beating occasionally or till all butter is melted completely. Stir in chopped rosemary, salt and black pepper and cook for 1 minute more. Pour sauce over lamb chops and serve.

Roasted Rack of Lamb

Makes: 4 servings

Ingredients:

- ¼ cup olive oil, divided
- 1 (7-bone) trimmed rack of lamb
- Salt and freshly ground black pepper, as required
- 2 tablespoons minced fresh rosemary
- 2 tablespoons minced garlic
- ½ cup fresh bread crumbs
- 1 tablespoon Dijon mustard

Procedure:

Preheat the oven to 450 degrees F. Place the rack in center of oven. In a large oven proof skillet, heat 2 tablespoons of oil on medium-high heat.

Add chops rack. Sprinkle with a little salt and black pepper. Sear the lamb rack for 1 to 2 minutes per side. Transfer the chops rack into a large plate. Keep aside for about 5 minutes to cool.

Meanwhile in a bowl, mix together remaining oil, rosemary, garlic, bread crumbs, salt and black pepper. Keep aside. Coat the chops rack with mustard evenly.
Then roll the chops rack in breadcrumbs mixture evenly. Cover the tips of bones with foil paper. Place the chops rack in the skillet. Roast for 12 to 18 minutes. Remove the chops rack from oven. Let it cool for about 6 to 7 minutes before slicing between the ribs.

Roasted Lamb Shank with Mashed Potatoes

Makes: 6 servings

Ingredients:

For Lamb Shanks:
- 6 (1½-pound) trimmed lamb shanks
- 4-5 sliced garlic cloves
- ½ cup fresh lime juice
- 2 teaspoons crushed dried marjoram
- 2 teaspoons crushed dried thyme
- Salt and freshly ground black pepper, as required
- 2 cups melted unsalted butter
- 12 unpeeled shallots
- 2 tablespoons minced fresh parsley

For Mashed Potatoes:
- 2 pounds peeled and cubed Yukon gold potatoes
- 1/3 cup warmed cream
- 3 tablespoons melted butter
- 2 tablespoons milk
- Salt and freshly ground black pepper, as needed

Procedure:

With the tip of a sharp knife, make cuts in several places. Press the garlic slices in each slit. In a large baking dish, place lamb shanks.

Drizzle with lemon juice. In a bowl, mix together marjoram, thyme, salt and black pepper. Rub the shanks with herb mixture evenly. Cover the dish and keep aside for at least 1 hour.

Preheat the oven to 500 degrees F. Place a covered ovenproof pan in the oven for at least 30 minutes. Remove shanks from marinade. Reserve the marinade.

Carefully, remove the pan from oven. Immediately place the shanks in the pan. Drizzle with melted butter. Place the pan in the oven. Place the lid of pan in another rack to keep it hot. Roast for about 25 minutes. Remove the pan from oven. Meanwhile in a small pan, add ½ cup water and reserved marinade on medium heat. Bring to a boil and pour hot marinade mixture over shanks. Add shallots with shanks.

Place a large foil paper over pan and cover with hot lid. Reduce the temperature of oven to 350 degrees F. roast for about 45 minutes.

Now, reduce the temperature of oven to 200 degrees F. Roast for about 20 minutes more. In a large pan of salted water, add potatoes. Bring to a boil on high heat. Reduce the heat to medium-low.

Cook for about 15 to 20 minutes or till done completely. Drain the potatoes and transfer into a large bowl. Add cream and butter and mash completely. Stir in milk, salt and black pepper.

Serve shanks wit gravy and mashed potatoes. Top with parsley and serve.

Grilled Spicy Lamb Chops

Makes: 2-4 servings

Ingredients:

- 2 tablespoons olive oil
- ¼ cup fresh lemon juice
- 2 teaspoons minced garlic
- ½ teaspoon minced fresh thyme
- ½ teaspoon minced fresh rosemary
- ¼ teaspoon ground cumin
- ¼ teaspoon cayenne pepper
- ¼ teaspoon crushed red pepper flakes
- Salt and freshly ground black pepper, as needed
- 4 (¾-inch thick) lamb chops

Procedure:

In a large bowl, mix together oil, lemon juice, garlic, thyme, rosemary, cumin, cayenne, red pepper flakes, salt and black pepper. Add chops and coat with marinade generously. Cover and refrigerator to marinate for about 6 to 8 hours.

Remove from refrigerate and keep in room temperature for at least 30 minutes. Preheat the grill to medium-high heat. Grease the grill grate. Cook for about 3½ minutes per side.

Grilled Chops with Cherry Tomatoes & Asparagus

Makes: 8 servings

Ingredients:

- ¼ cup olive oil
- ¼ cup balsamic vinegar
- 2 tablespoons fresh lemon juice
- 3-4 minced garlic cloves
- 2 teaspoons crushed dried rosemary
- Salt and freshly ground black pepper, as required
- 8 (1-inch thick) lamb chops

For Cherry Tomatoes & Asparagus:
- 32 fresh stemmed cherry tomatoes
- 1½ pounds trimmed asparagus
- 3 tablespoons olive oil
- 2 teaspoons minced fresh parsley
- 2 teaspoons minced fresh rosemary
- Salt and freshly ground black pepper, as required

Procedure:

In a large bowl, mix together oil, vinegar, lemon juice, garlic, rosemary, salt and black pepper. Add chops and coat with marinade generously.

Cover and refrigerate to marinate for about 4 to 5 hours. Remove from refrigerator and keep in room temperature for at least 30 minutes. Preheat the grill to medium-high heat. Grease the grill grate. Cook for about 4 minutes per side.

Remove grill and transfer into a large plate. Cover with foil paper to keep them warm. Meanwhile for vegetables in a large bowl, add all ingredients and toss to coat well. Thread the cherry tomatoes onto presoaked wooden skewers.

After removing chops from grill, grease the grill grate again. Place the skewers on grill and cook for 3 to 4 minutes per side.

After that increase the temperature of grill to high heat. Grill the asparagus for about 2 to 3 minutes. Divide the chops tomatoes and asparagus in 8 serving plates evenly and serve.

Grilled Leg of Lamb

Makes: 8 servings

Ingredients:

- 4 minced large garlic cloves
- 2 tablespoons minced fresh thyme
- 1 teaspoon finely grated lemon zest
- ¼ cup fresh lemon juice
- ½ cup olive oil
- Salt and freshly ground black pepper, as required
- 1 (4½-pound) trimmed and butter flied boneless leg of lamb

Procedure:

In a large bowl, mix together garlic, thyme, lemon zest, lemon juice, oil, salt and black pepper. Add leg of lamb and coat with marinade generously.

Cover and refrigerate to marinate for about 6 to 8 hours, turning often. Remove from refrigerator and keep in room temperature for at least 1 hour. Prepare the grill over direct heat on medium-high heat. Generously, grease the grill grate.

Remove leg of lamb from bowl and discard the extra marinade. Take 3 or 4 metal skewers and run lengthwise through the leg of lamb about 1½-2 inches apart. Cook for about 10 to 14 minutes, flipping occasionally.

Transfer the leg of lamb to a cutting board, remove the skewers and cover with a foil paper for 20 minutes before slicing. With a sharp knife, cut the lamb across the grain in desired size slices.

Lamb & Carrot Soup

Makes: 8 servings

Ingredients:

- 2 pounds trimmed and cubed boneless lamb shoulder
- 1 teaspoon ground cinnamon
- ¼ teaspoon ground ginger
- ¼ teaspoon ground nutmeg
- Salt and freshly ground black pepper, as required
- 2 tablespoons olive oil
- 1 thinly sliced medium onion
- 2 chopped celery stalks
- 3 peeled and cubed large carrots
- 6 minced garlic cloves
- 1 bay leaf
- 1 cup red wine
- 1 cup chicken broth
- 1 (28-ounce) can diced tomatoes (with liquid)
- ¼ cup chopped fresh thyme

Procedure:

In a large bowl, add lamb, cinnamon, ginger, nutmeg, salt and black pepper and toss to coat well. Refrigerate, covered to marinate for at least 8 to 12 hours.

In a large soup pan, heat oil on medium heat. Add lamb and cook for about 4 to 5 minutes. Add onion, celery and carrot and cook for about 4 to 5 minutes more.

Add garlic and bay leaf and cook for 1 minute more. Stir in red wine and diced tomatoes with juice and bring to a boil. Then reduce the heat to low. Cover and simmer for about 2 hours or till desired doneness. Stir in thyme and serve hot.

Lamb & Beans Soup

Makes: 8 servings

Ingredients:

- 3 tablespoons olive oil
- 1 chopped medium onion
- 2 chopped celery stalks
- 2 peeled and chopped medium carrots
- 2-3 minced garlic cloves
- 1 teaspoon crushed dried oregano
- 1 teaspoon crushed dried thyme
- 1¼ pounds lean ground lamb
- 1½ cups canned Roma tomatoes (with liquid)
- ½ pound soaked for overnight and drained great northern
- Beans
- 6 cups chicken broth
- ½ pound fresh baby spinach
- Salt and freshly ground black pepper, as required

Procedure:

In a large soup pan, heat oil on medium heat. Add onion, celery and carrot and sauté for about 4 to 5 minutes. Add garlic, oregano and thyme and sauté for 1 minute more. Add lamb and cook for about 4 to 5 minutes.

Stir in tomatoes, beans and broth and bring to a boil on high heat. Then reduce the heat to low. Simmer, covered for about 1½ hours or till beans become tender. Stir in spinach, salt and black pepper and cook for 4 to 5 minutes further.

Serve hot.

Lamb & Beans Soup

Makes: 4-5 servings

Ingredients:

- 2 tablespoons olive oil
- 1 pound cubed lamb stew meat
- Salt and freshly ground black pepper, as required
- 1 large peeled and chopped turnip
- 2 medium peeled and chopped carrots
- 1 large chopped onion
- 2/3 cup pearl barley
- 1 (12-ounce) bottle beer
- 3 (14-ounce) cans beef broth
- ½ teaspoon crushed dried thyme
- ½ teaspoon crushed dried rosemary
- 1 tablespoon fresh lemon juice
- 2 tablespoons chopped fresh parsley

Procedure:

In a large pan, heat oil on medium heat. Add lamb and sprinkle with salt and black pepper. Cook for about 4 to 5 minutes or till browned from all sides.

Transfer the lamb into a crock pot. Place turnip, carrots and onion over cooked lamb. Add barley, beer, broth, thyme and rosemary and stir to combine.

Set the crock pot on low. Cover and cook for about 8 to 10 hours. Turn off the crock pot and remove the lid of crock pot. Stir in lemon juice. Serve hot with the garnishing of parsley.

Spicy Minced Lamb with Peas

Makes: 6 servings

Ingredients:

- 2 tablespoons extra virgin olive oil
- 1 pound lean ground lamb
- 1 large finely chopped white onion
- 2 minced medium cloves
- ½ tablespoon minced fresh ginger
- 1 teaspoon ground coriander
- 1 teaspoon ground cumin
- ¼ teaspoon chili powder
- ¼ teaspoon ground turmeric
- 2 medium seeded and chopped tomatoes
- ½ cup chicken broth
- Salt and freshly ground black pepper, as required
- 2¼ cups shelled frozen peas
- 2 tablespoons sliced almonds
- 2 tablespoons chopped fresh cilantro

Procedure:

In a large skillet, heat oil on medium heat. Add lamb and cook stirring for about 4-5 minutes or till browned completely.

Transfer the lamb into a large bowl. In the same skillet, add onion and sauté for about 4 to 5 minutes. Add garlic, ginger, coriander, cumin, chili powder, turmeric, and sauté for about 1 minute or till aromatic.

Add tomatoes and cook for about 2 to 3 minutes, crushing completely with the back of spoon. Stir in the lamb and broth and bring to a boil. Then reduce the heat to medium-low. Cook covered, stirring often for about 8-10 minutes.

Stir in peas and cook for 15-20 minutes. Remove from heat and serve hot with the garnishing of almonds and cilantro leaves.

Baked Spicy Meatballs with Yogurt Dip

Makes: 6-8 servings

Ingredients:

For Meatballs:
- 1 pound lean ground lamb
- ¼ cup very finely chopped onion
- 1 minced garlic clove
- 1 tablespoon chopped fresh mint
- 1 tablespoon chopped fresh cilantro
- ¼ teaspoon ground cinnamon
- ½ teaspoon ground cumin
- ½ teaspoon cayenne pepper
- Salt and freshly ground black pepper, as required

For Yogurt Dip:
- 1 cup plain Greek yogurt
- 1 teaspoon ground cumin
- 2 teaspoons minced fresh mint
- 2 teaspoons minced fresh cilantro

Procedure:

Preheat the oven to 375 degrees F. Place the rack in the middle of oven. Grease a large baking sheet. For meatballs in a large bowl, add ground lamb, onion, garlic, mint leaves, cilantro leaves, cinnamon, cumin, cayenne pepper, salt and black pepper and combine till well combined.

Keep aside for 15 to 20 minutes. Make small equal sized balls from mixture. Arrange the meatballs in prepared baking sheet in a single layer. Bake for about 15 minutes or till desired doneness.

For yogurt dip in a medium bowl, add yogurt, cumin, mint leaves and cilantro leaves and mix till well combined. Serve meatballs with yogurt dip and enjoy.

Meatballs in Spicy Tomato Gravy

Makes: 6 servings

Ingredients:

For Meatballs:
- 1 pound lean ground lamb
- 1 tablespoon tomato paste
- ¼ cup chopped fresh coriander leaves
- 1 finely chopped small onion
- 2 minced small garlic cloves
- ½ teaspoon ground cumin
- Salt and freshly ground black pepper, to taste

For Tomato Gravy:
- 3 tablespoons extra-virgin olive oil, divided
- 2 finely chopped medium onions
- 2 finely minced large garlic cloves
- ½ tablespoon minced fresh ginger
- 1 teaspoon crushed dried thyme
- teaspoon ground cinnamon
- ½ teaspoon ground cumin
- 1 teaspoon cayenne pepper
- ¼ teaspoon ground turmeric
- 3 finely chopped large tomatoes
- Salt and freshly ground black pepper, to taste
- 1½ cups warm chicken broth

Procedure:

For meatballs in a large bowl, add ground lamb, tomato paste, cilantro leaves, onion, garlic, cumin, salt and black pepper and combine till well combined. Keep aside.

For tomato gravy heat 1 tablespoon of oil in a large pan on medium heat. Add meatballs and cook for about 4 to 5 minutes or till lightly browned from all sides.

In the same pan, heat remaining oil on medium heat. Add onion and sauté for about 8 to 10 minutes. Add garlic, ginger, thyme, cinnamon, cumin, cayenne pepper and turmeric and sauté for about 1 minute.

Add tomatoes and cook for about 3-4 minutes, crushing with the back of spoon or till oil starts to separate from the mixture. Add warm broth and bring to a boil.

Carefully add meatballs and cook without stirring for 5 minutes. Reduce the heat to low. Cover the pan partially and cook for about 15 to 20 minutes, stirring carefully 2 to 3 times or till the desired thickness of gravy and meatballs are done completely.

Cheesy Lamb Burgers with Mayo Dip

Makes: 8 servings

Ingredients:

For Mayo Dip:
- ¼ cup minced scallion
- 1 minced small garlic clove
- ¼ cup extra-virgin olive oil
- 2 cups mayonnaise

For Lamb Burgers:
- 1½ pounds lean ground lamb
- ¼ cup chopped onion
- 2 tablespoons minced cilantro leaves
- 4-ounce shredded cheddar cheese
- 2/3 cup fat-free evaporated milk
- ½ cup dry bread crumbs
- 1 teaspoon prepared mustard
- Salt and freshly ground black pepper, to taste

For Serving:
- Fresh lettuce leaves

Procedure:

For dip in a food processor, add scallion, garlic and oil and pulse till well combined. Add mayonnaise and pulse till well combined. Transfer the dip into a bowl.

Cover and refrigerate to chill before serving. Preheat the grill to medium heat. Grease the grill grate. In a large bowl, add ground lamb, onion, cilantro, cheese, milk, breadcrumbs, mustard, salt and black pepper and combine till well combined.

Make 8 equal sized patties from mixture. Grill for 5 to 6 minutes per side. Serve the burgers over the bed of lettuce with the topping of dip.

Two Awesome Free Gifts For You

I want to say "Thank You" for buying my book so I've put together a few, awesome free gifts for you.

The Essential Kitchen Series Cooking Hacks & Tips Book

&

100 Delicious New Recipes

These gifts are the perfect add-on to this book and I know you'll love them.

So visit the link below to grab them now!

www.GoodLivingPublishing.com/essential-kitchen

Copyright DT FUTURES INC PUBLISHING. All rights reserved.

This book is copyright protected and intended for personal use only. You may not amend, distribute, sell, use, quote, or paraphrase any part of or any content within this book without the full consent of the author, publishing company, and/or copyright owner. Making copies of these pages or any portion for any purpose other than your personal use is a violation of United States copyright laws.

Disclaimer

DT Futures Inc Publishing and its authors have used their best efforts in preparing these pages and their publications. DT Futures Inc Publishing and its authors make no warranty of any kind, expressed or implied, with regard to the information supplied.

Limits of Liability

DT Futures Publishing and its authors shall not be liable in the event of incidental or consequential damages in connection with, or arising out of, the providing of the information offered here.

Printed in Great Britain
by Amazon